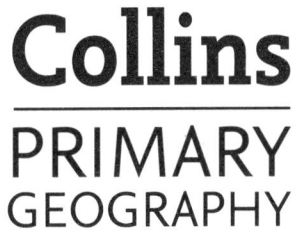

Change
Workbook 5

Planet Earth	**Seas and oceans**	
	Beneath the surface	2
	The ocean environment	4
	Learning about seas	6
Water	**Wearing away the land**	
	Rivers in action	8
	Preventing flood damage	10
	Finding out about rivers	12
Weather	**The seasons**	
	Changing seasons	14
	Seasons worldwide	16
	Seasonal influences	18
Settlements	**Cities**	
	Describing cities	20
	World cities	22
	The story of London	24
Work and Travel	**Jobs**	
	Making things	26
	Different jobs	28
	Types of work	30
Environment	**Pollution**	
	Damaging the environment	32
	'Green living'	34
	Exploring clean energy	36
Places	**Wales**	38
	Greece	44
	North America	50
	Africa	56

Daphne Paizee

Unit 1 Seas and oceans

Lesson 1: Beneath the surface

1 Complete the sentences. Use the words from the boxes.

| minerals | volcanoes | deep | trenches | vents |

a) Some animals that live in the sea get food from _____ that are pumped into the ocean from the _____ under the water.

b) There are more _____ under the ocean than on dry land. There are also _____, which are long, narrow ditches. These can be very _____.

2 a) Find out where the creatures in these photographs live. Write the phrases under the photographs.

| near the surface | on the ocean floor |

Hint: More than one phrase might work for some of the photos.

starfish: _____

coral: _____

dolphins: _____

lobster: _____

b) Some creatures need to breathe in air. Which of the creatures in the photographs needs air? Why do you think so?

_____

_____

Unit 1 Seas and oceans

3 This picture shows some animals and plants that live in different places below the ocean. Complete the picture by drawing more animals and plants.

- Think about where the plants could grow.
- Use colours to show which parts are colder and deeper.

Unit 1 Seas and oceans

Lesson 2: The ocean environment

❶ Look at the photograph. Explain why the ship, which is carrying oil, may threaten the oceans.

_____

❷ Make a list of three other threats to the ocean.

_____   _____   _____

❸ Read these statements. <u>Underline</u> two sentences with incorrect information. Write the information correctly below.

- Oceans help to create different climates.
- Ocean currents take cold water from hot tropical areas around the equator to warmer parts of the world.
- Ocean currents move cold water from the polar areas back to the Tropics.
- Global warming cannot change the climate of an area.

_____

_____

4

Unit 1 **Seas and oceans**

4 Look at these photographs. They show threats to the ocean environment.

a) Write a caption to explain what you see in each photograph.

b) Find or draw pictures in the boxes below to show other threats.

→ Supports Pupil Book Investigation, page 5

Unit 1 Seas and oceans

Lesson 3: Learning about seas

1 Are these seas or oceans? Complete the names with the word Sea or Ocean.

Mediterranean _____   North _____

Pacific _____   Indian _____

Caribbean _____   Red _____

2 Read the clues and complete the crossword puzzle.

Clues across

3   These swim around in the ocean and sea and are an important source of food.

5   The North Sea is famous for pumping oil from one of these.

Clues down

1   This is a natural resource which we can use to make clean electricity.

2   Most water in the North Sea can be described as this. It is the opposite of deep.

4   People mine and extract this fossil fuel resource from the seabed.

3 What can visitors do to enjoy themselves at the seaside? Make a short list of activities.

_____

_____

_____

Unit 1 Seas and oceans

4 Complete this paragraph about the North Sea. Use the words from the boxes.

| fish stocks | oil | Norway | resources | wind | shores | Forth |

The North Sea lies between the United Kingdom, France, Netherlands, Belgium, Denmark, _____ and Germany. Rivers such as the _____ and the Rhine flow into the sea. Millions of people live on the _____ and visit the sea, which is also the natural habitat of seals, whales, fish, birds and many other animals. It is one of the busiest seas in the world. The sea provides natural _____ such as _____ and gas. _____ farms provide renewable energy. All these activities have resulted in heavy pollution. _____, which were once plentiful, have grown smaller.

5 Add symbols to this map to show wind farms in the North Sea.

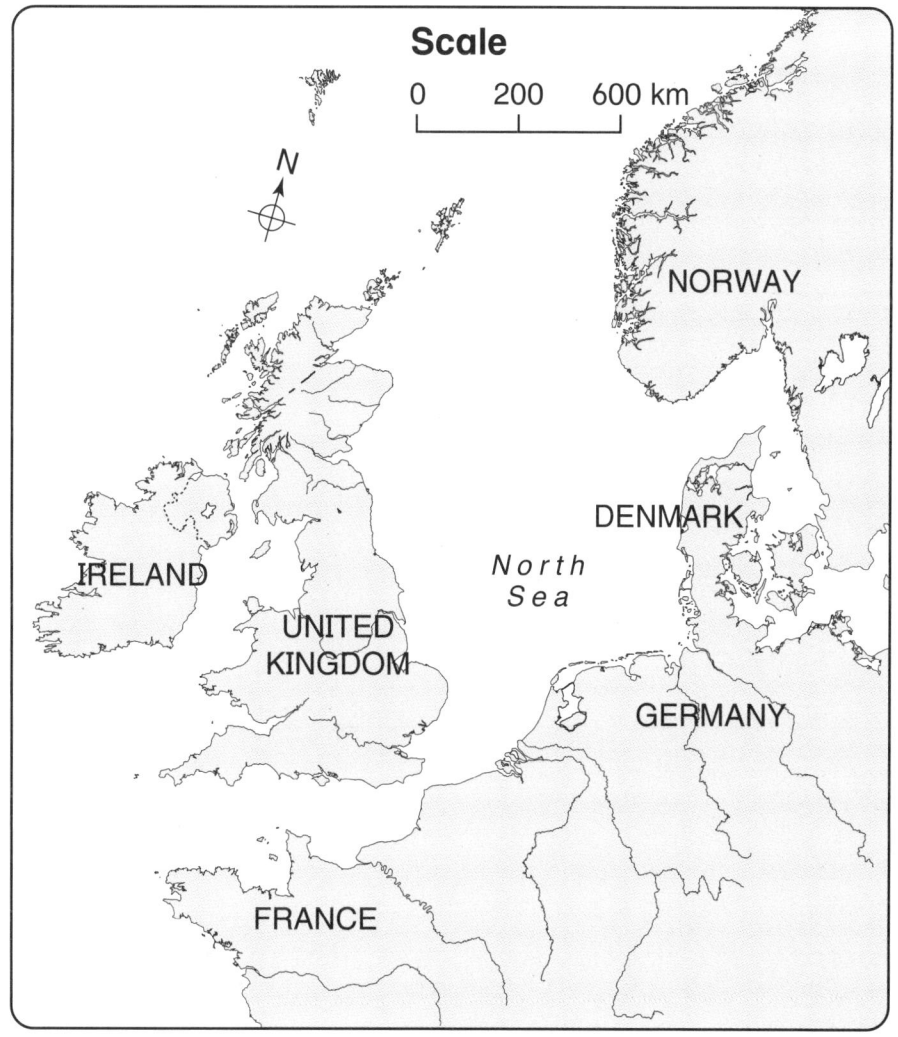

→ Supports Pupil Book Mapwork, page 7

Unit 2 Wearing away the land

Lesson 1: Rivers in action

1 One of these statements about rivers is false. <u>Underline</u> the statement. Write the sentence correctly below.

- Rivers flow downhill, in channels, and sometimes with a lot of force.
- The amount of water in the world is always the same.
- Rivers can wear down and build up areas of land.
- The sides of a river cut into the river banks.
- Material carried by the water in rivers is always deposited in lakes.
- The way that water moves round the world is called the water cycle.

_____

_____

2 a) Explain two ways in which a river can *wear down* the land.

_____

_____

_____

_____

b) Explain how a river can *build up* the land.

_____

_____

_____

_____

_____

Unit 2 Wearing away the land

3 Read the headings above these pictures. Then colour in the pictures to show the water clearly.

4 Write a definition for each word, like one that would appear in a dictionary.

> **Hint:** Use your own words in your definitions. You could create your own Geography key vocabulary dictionary in a notebook.

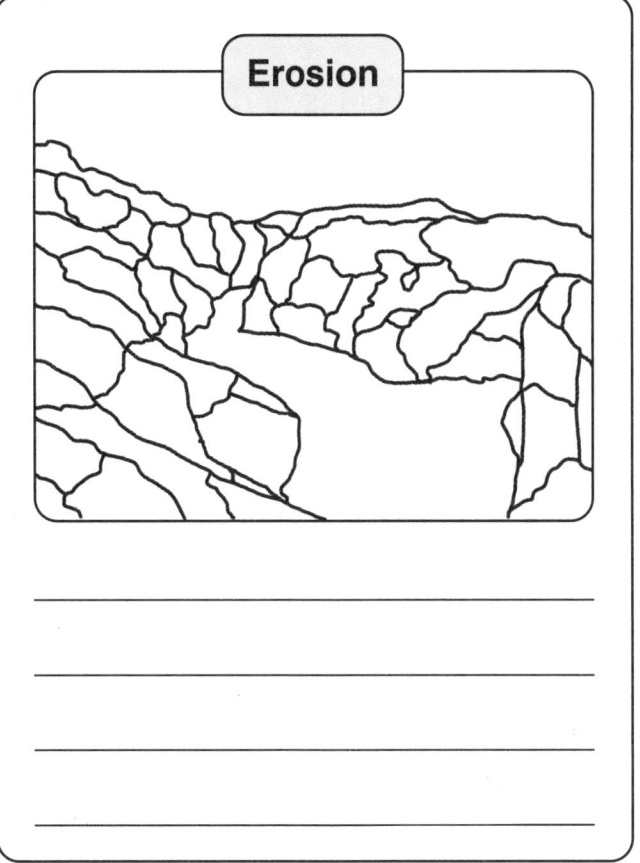

Erosion

_____
_____
_____
_____

Deposition

_____
_____
_____

Transportation

_____
_____
_____

→ Supports Pupil Book Investigation, page 9

Unit 2 Wearing away the land

Lesson 2: Preventing flood damage

1 Read these clues and find the words in the wordsearch puzzle.

a) Clay bank on the sides of a river which holds back water when the river floods. l _ _ _ _

b) The route taken by water in a river. c _ _ _ _ _ _

c) A bend in a river. m _ _ _ _ _ _

d) This happens when there is too much rain and a river overflows. f _ _ _ _

e) These are made of concrete and are placed on the sides and bottoms of a river channel to make it stronger. b _ _ _ _

f) This is made on a meander to allow the water to flow faster. c _ _ o _ _

g) A wall built on one side of a river to stop flooding and force the river to make a deeper channel on the other side. d _ _ _

c	e	u	x	c	o	h	t	d
h	r	i	b	u	t	a	r	y
a	l	c	o	t	z	y	g	k
n	e	s	x	o	w	b	p	e
n	v	z	e	f	l	o	o	d
e	e	f	s	f	i	v	l	q
l	e	m	e	a	n	d	e	r

2 Answer these questions.

a) Imagine you are the captain of a riverboat on the Mississippi River in the United States more than 100 years ago. What dangers will you look out for?

_____

_____

b) Name two things that were done to make the Mississippi River safer.

_____

_____

Unit 2 Wearing away the land

❸ Draw the Mississippi River and its **tributary**, the Missouri River, on this map of the United States.

> **Hint:** A **tributary** is a river or stream that flows into a bigger river or lake. The Missouri River rises in the Rocky Mountains and joins the Mississippi at St Louis, before flowing down to the sea.

Colour the water shown on the map in blue.

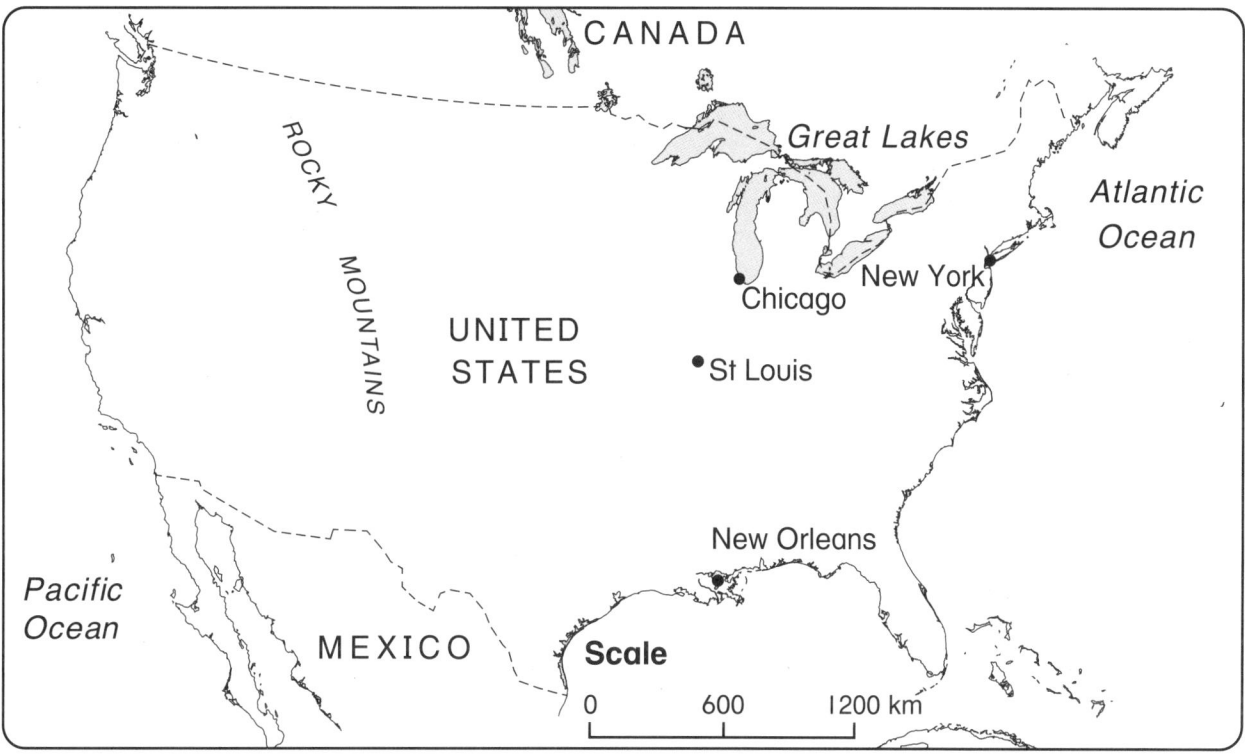

❹ Look at this photograph of a town near the Tha Chin River in Thailand. What happened? What did people do?

_____

_____

Unit 2 — Wearing away the land

Lesson 3: Finding out about rivers

1 a) This person has collected river water in a tube. What might she be able to find out about the river from this sample?

Hint: Which of the river survey questions on Pupil Book page 12 will she be able to investigate?

b) Why has this measuring stick been placed in the water?

Unit 2   Wearing away the land

❷ Make a list of six pieces of equipment you need to conduct a survey of a river. Explain briefly what you would do with each piece of equipment. Look at the example.

Equipment	How you could use it to collect data
Plastic collecting bottle	*To see if there are any particles carried in the water*

→ Supports Pupil Book Investigation, page 13

Unit 3 The seasons

Lesson 1: Changing seasons

1 What season does each photograph show? How do you know?
Look for clues and write your answer under each photograph.

_____
_____
_____
_____

_____
_____
_____
_____

_____
_____
_____
_____

_____
_____
_____
_____

Unit 3 **The seasons**

2 Read the temperature chart and answer the questions.

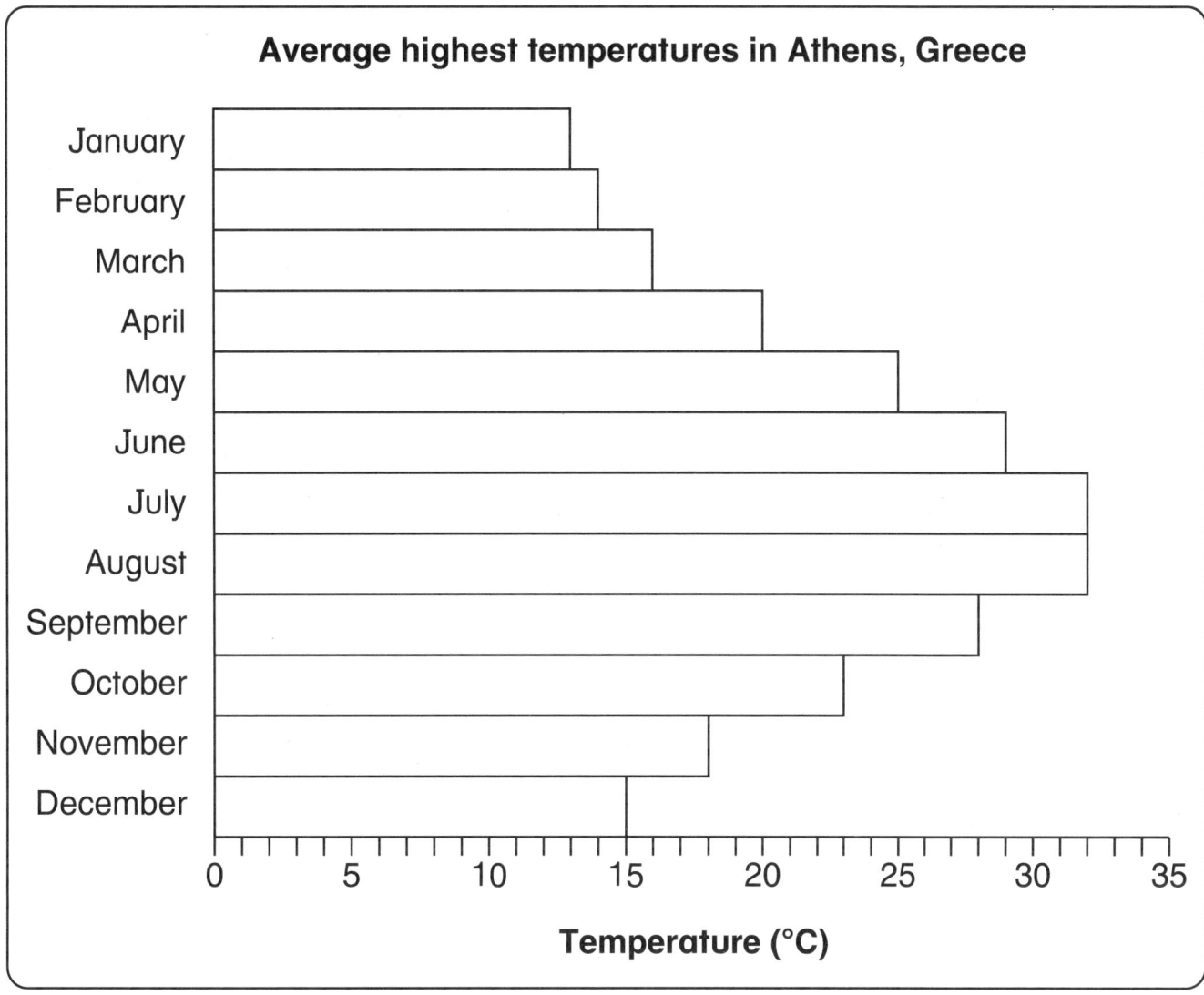

a) Which are the summer months in Athens?

_____

b) During which months would you need a coat on a visit to Athens?

_____

c) In June 2024, some outdoor tourist attractions in Athens were closed because the highest daytime temperatures were over 40°C. What do you think caused these very high temperatures?

_____

d) Find out what the temperature is today in Athens. Compare the temperature to the temperature for that month on the chart. Is it different? Can you suggest why?

_____

Unit 3 The seasons

Lesson 2: Seasons worldwide

1 This diagram shows the seasons in southern Europe. Look at the information and answer the questions.

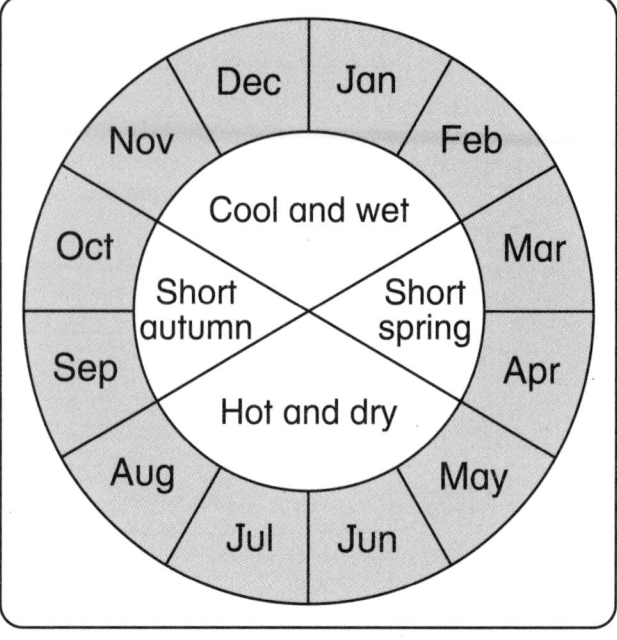

a) What kind of climate does southern Europe have?

_____

_____

b) Name two countries in Europe that have a climate like this.

_____

_____

c) Which are the winter months?

_____

_____

_____

d) Write a full sentence to describe what it is like in summer.

_____

_____

2 What type of climate do cities such as Mumbai and Hong Kong have?

_____

3 a) What is the weather like when a monsoon rain starts?

_____

b) Why are monsoon rains important?

_____

_____

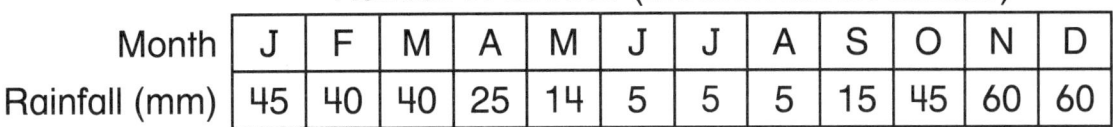

Unit 3 — The seasons

4 Use the information below to create a rainfall chart for Greece.

Rainfall in Greece (Mediterranean climate)

Month	J	F	M	A	M	J	J	A	S	O	N	D
Rainfall (mm)	45	40	40	25	14	5	5	5	15	45	60	60

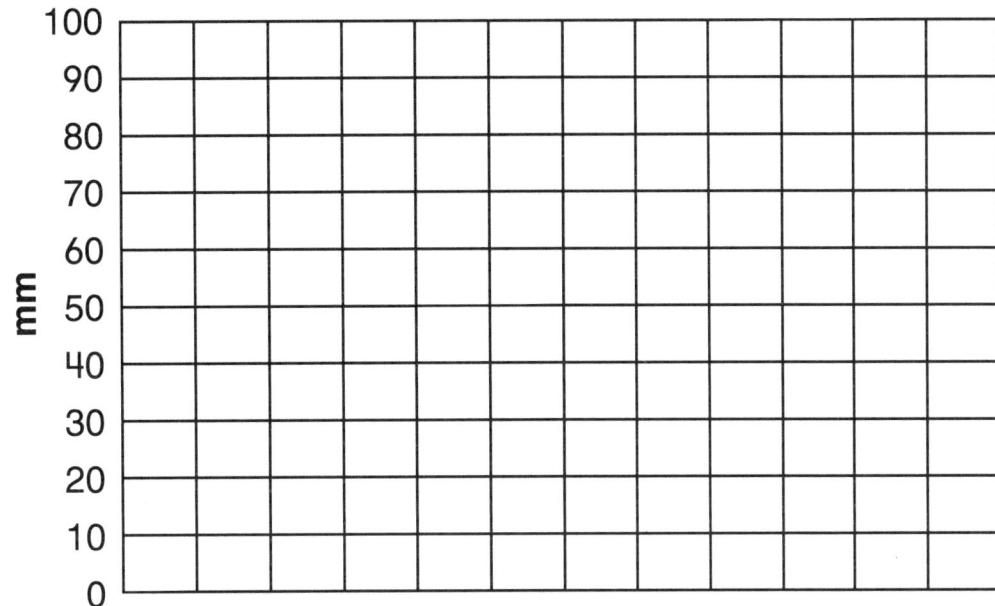

5 a) Complete the diagram to show the cycle of seasons where you live.

b) Write a description of the weather in one season where you live. Do not name the season. Here are some example sentence starters.

This is a time of year when …

During the day it is …

People like to …

The temperature …

Animals need …

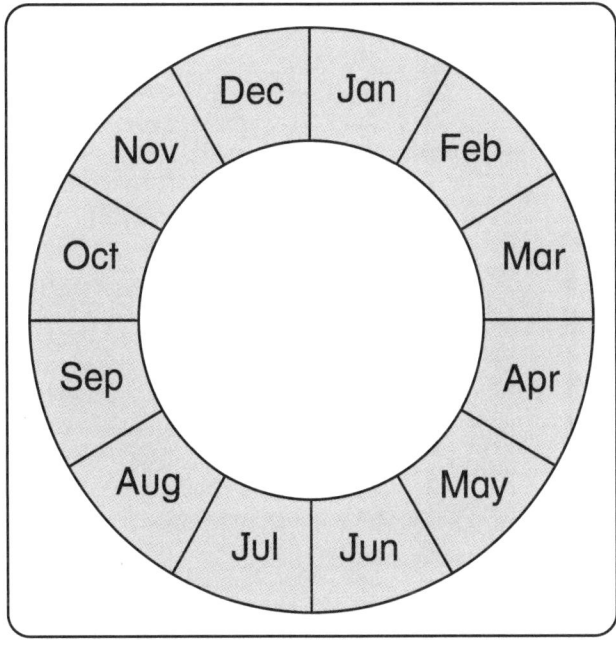

→ Supports Pupil Book Investigation, page 17

Unit 3 The seasons

Lesson 3: Seasonal influences

1 Look at these two photographs. They show dairy farms in Switzerland during different seasons.

a) Name the season shown in each picture.

b) Write a sentence to describe what the farmers have to do to look after the cows in that season.

cows in a barn

Season: _____

Farmer's job: _____

cows grazing on grass in the mountains

Season: _____

Farmer's job: _____

Unit 3   **The seasons**

❷ How do different seasons affect your life? Draw pictures and write notes to answer these questions.

a) How do you keep warm when it is cold?	
b) What can you do during summer school holidays?	
c) How do you travel to school when it is raining?	
d) What plants can you see in spring?	

Unit 4   Cities

Lesson 1: Describing cities

1 Answer these questions to describe a city. Write in full sentences.

a) Is a city a big or small settlement?	
b) What types of buildings are there in the centre of a city?	
c) What can people do during the day?	
d) What can people do at night?	
e) How do people get from one place to another?	
f) Why do many people choose to live in the suburbs of a city?	

2 Why do some people not enjoy living in a city? Give two reasons.

Unit 4 Cities

❸ Use an atlas to help you sketch an outline map of the country where you live. Write the names of five cities on the map.

Unit 4 Cities

Lesson 2: World cities

1 Write five interesting facts that you have learnt about the city of New York.

_____

_____

_____

_____

_____

2 Use the data in the table. Draw a bar chart to show the population of the ten biggest cities in the world in 2020.

- Write the names of the cities.
- Colour in the columns to show the population in millions.

City	People (millions) 2020
Tokyo, Japan	37
Delhi, India	30
Shanghai, China	27
Mumbai, India	20
Mexico City, Mexico	22
Cairo, Egypt	21
São Paulo, Brazil	22
Beijing, China	20
Dhaka, Bangladesh	21
Osaka, Japan	19

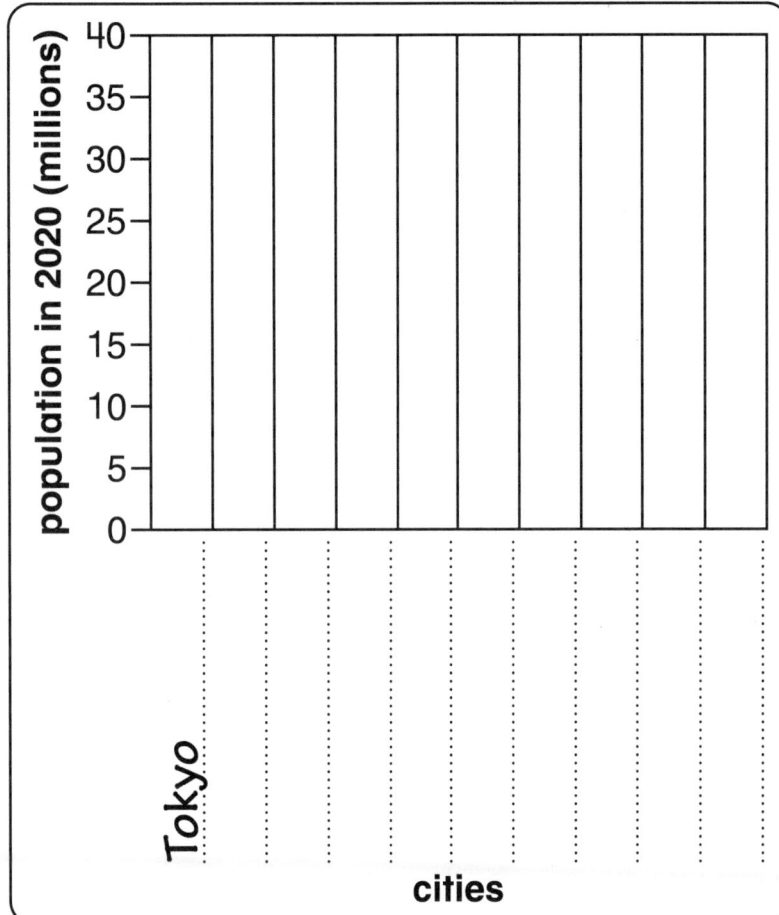

→ Supports Pupil Book Investigation, page 22

Unit 4 Cities

❸ The Statue of Liberty and the Hudson River are landmarks in New York. Use an atlas to complete the landmark labels on the map. Add any more landmarks you can find.

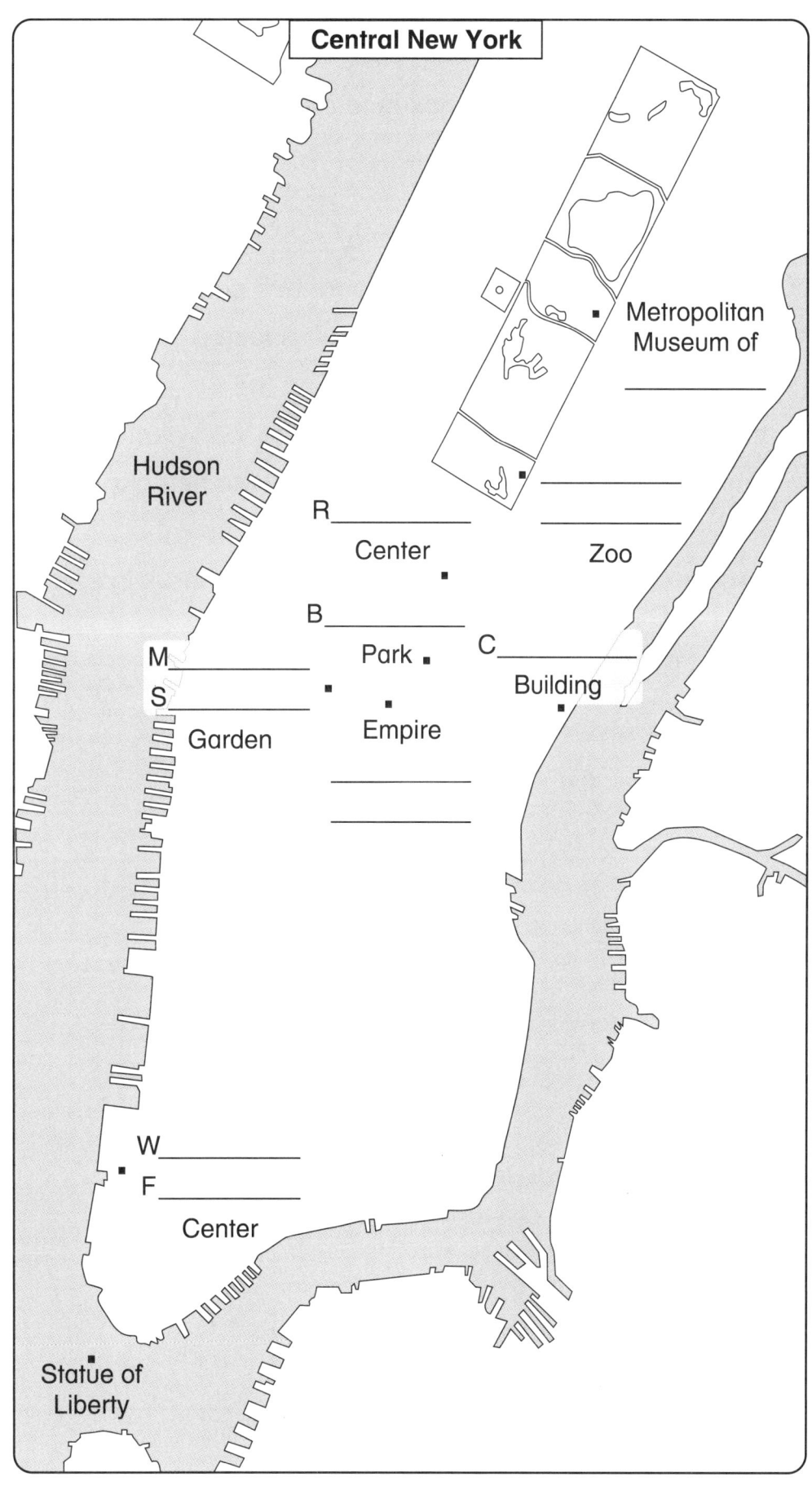

Central New York

Metropolitan Museum of _____

Hudson River

R_____ Center

_____ Zoo

B_____ Park

M_____
S_____ Garden

C_____ Building

Empire _____
_____

W_____
F_____ Center

Statue of Liberty

23

Unit 4 Cities

Lesson 3: The story of London

1 Use the words from the boxes to complete the paragraph about London.

| Great Fire | underground | Norman | crossing | Romans |

The city of London was built at a _____ point on the River Thames where boats could offload their cargo. The _____ built a wall around the city to protect it. It became a capital city during _____ times. In 1666 the _____ destroyed many of the buildings in the city. By the 19th century, London had become a big and prosperous city. London was the first city in the world to have _____ trains.

2 Draw or find a picture of an interesting landmark in London. Write a sentence to describe the landmark.

Unit 4   Cities

3 Which of the following are **cities** in the United Kingdom? Circle the names.

Glasgow   Cardiff   Mayfair   London

Thames   Belfast   Leeds

4 a) Look again at the tourist map of London on page 25 of your Pupil Book. Make a list of four of the landmarks from the map that you would like to visit.

_____   _____

_____   _____

b) Mark the four places on the street map of central London. Draw the route you could take to walk to these places. Start at the Strand.

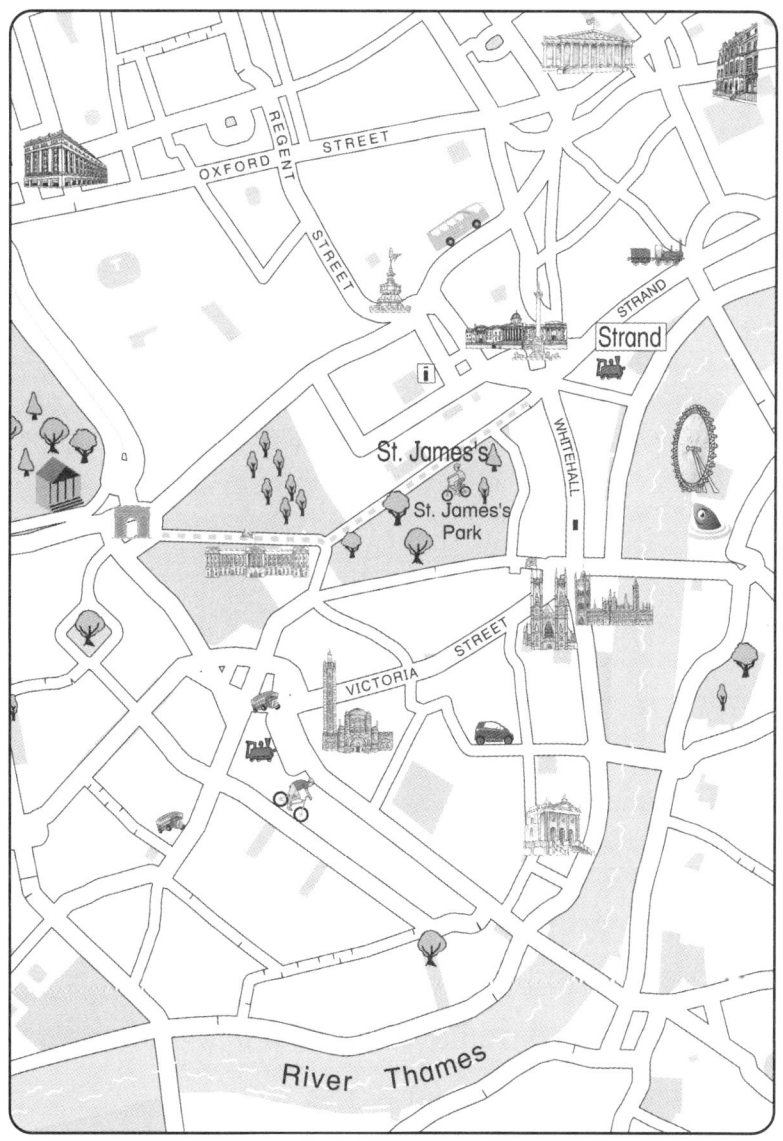

→ Supports Pupil Book Mapwork, page 25

Unit 5   Jobs

Lesson 1: Making things

1 a) Colour the empty boxes in the key below using the colours specified.

b) Complete the drawing to create a plan of a factory. Include the areas and items listed in the key. Use the rectangles for the different work areas.

c) Colour your plan using the colours from the key.

Work areas		Transport		Energy		Environment	
workshop		main entrance		boiler		trees	
offices		delivery area		chimney		grass	
storage space		car park				hedges	
Red		Yellow		Brown		Green	

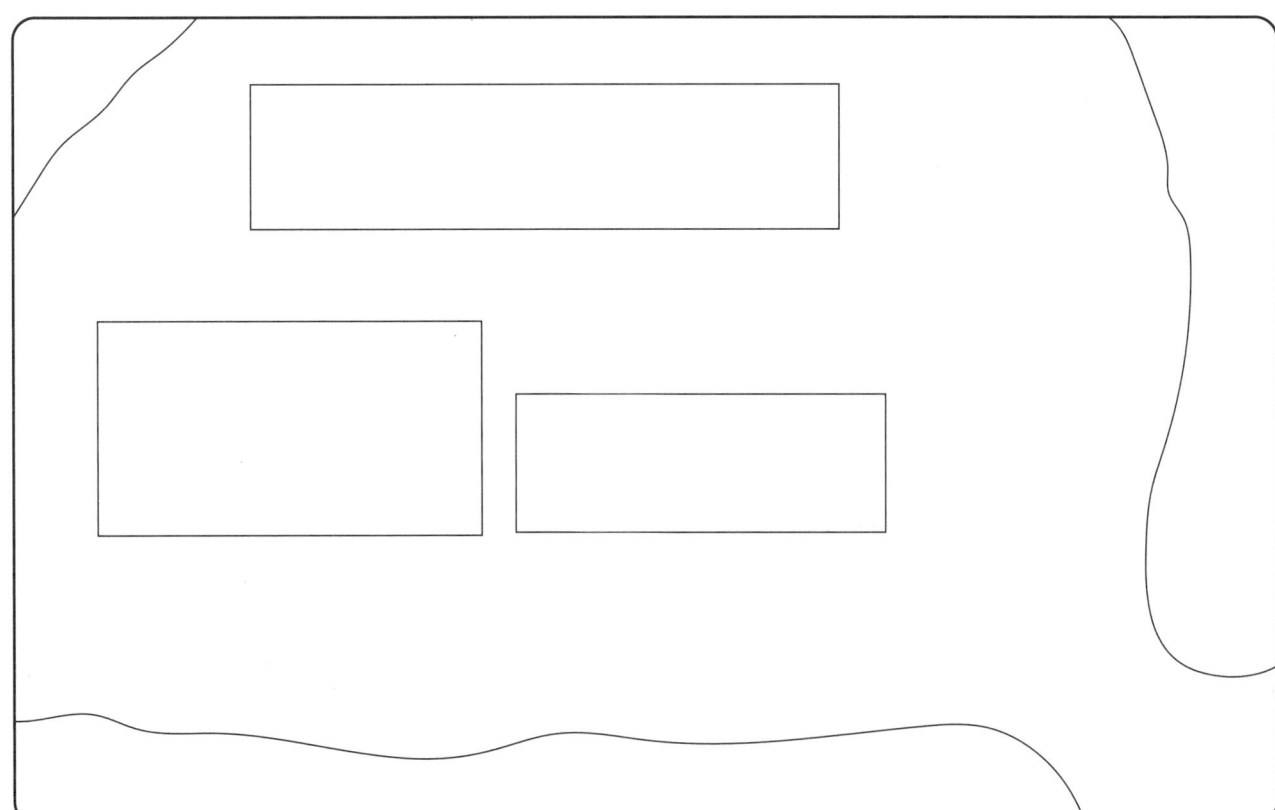

2 Which two statements about factories are true (T) and which are false (F)? Write T or F next to each statement.

a) Factories use machines to make goods quickly and cheaply. ____

b) Factories need thousands of employees. ____

c) Factories need power supplies for their machinery. ____

d) Everything that we eat and wear is made in a factory. ____

Unit 5 Jobs

❸ The pictures below show the different stages in the process of making apple juice.

a) The pictures are not in the correct order. Number the pictures correctly in the small boxes.

b) Write the raw materials next to 'Input' and the final goods next to 'Output'.

c) Write a short sentence to explain what happens at each stage.

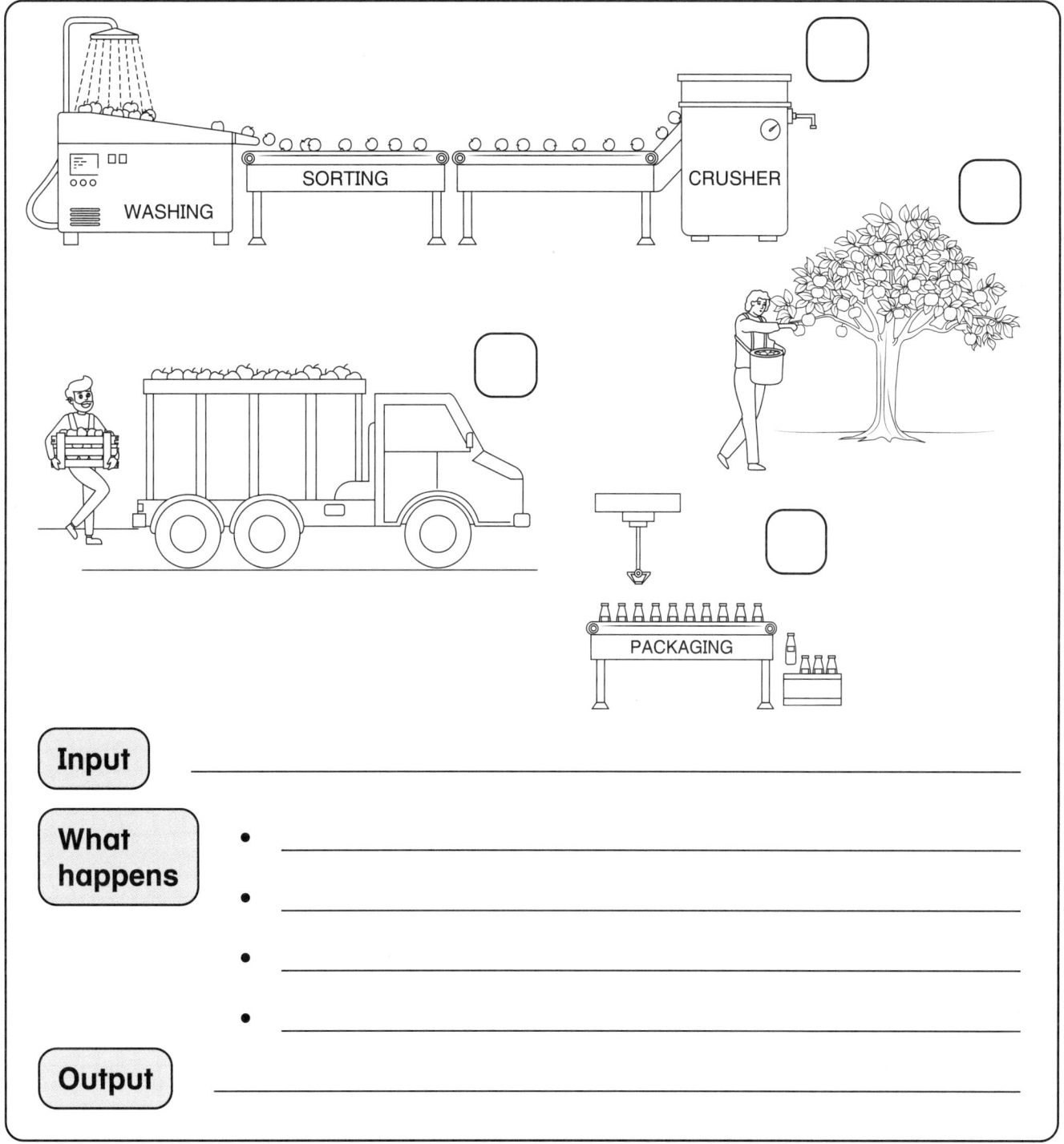

Input _____

What happens
- _____
- _____
- _____
- _____

Output _____

➜ Supports Pupil Book Investigation, page 27

Unit 5 Jobs

Lesson 2: Different jobs

1 The people in the table below all earn a living working in a harbour. To do their jobs, they need certain skills and knowledge. Choose skills from the word boxes that you think each person needs. Write the skills in the table.

- organised and good at planning
- understands food safety
- careful, precise and good with numbers
- brave and courageous
- knowledge of the engines on boats

Job	Special skills needed
Harbour master	
Engineer	
Boat captain	
Accountant	
Fish factory worker	

→ Supports Pupil Book Investigation, page 29

2 a) Which job do you think is the most important in a harbour? Why?

_____

_____

b) Which job would you most like to do? Why?

_____

_____

c) What type of technology would you need to use to be able to do this job?

_____

Unit 5 Jobs

❸ Look at the plan of a fishing harbour below. Use ideas from this example to help you create a plan of the harbour shown in the picture on pages 28 and 29 of your Pupil Book. Your plan should include:

- a place for boats to move around
- places for boats to load and unload
- roads for trucks
- factories
- offices.

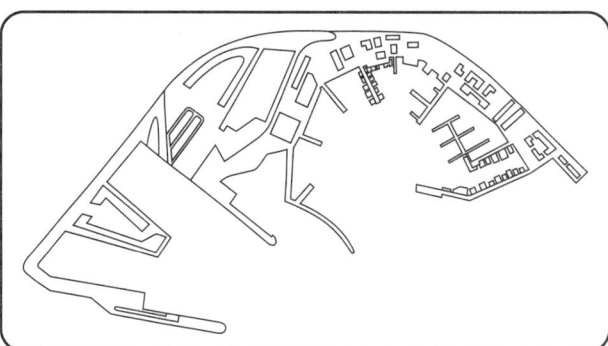

→ Supports Pupil Book Mapwork, page 29

Unit 5   Jobs

Lesson 3: Types of work

❶ Complete the diagram below using the labels from the box. Draw or find a picture to give an example of each type of activity.

| primary | secondary | tertiary |

```
                    Types of
                   activities
```

_____ activities

_____ activities

_____ activities

❷ How can technology and artificial intelligence change primary activities?

Use your example of a primary activity and explain how this job could change.

For example:

Forestry: cutting down trees

Woodcutters used axes and saws to chop down trees. With new technology, machines can cut down trees more quickly and easily. This means that woodcutters need to learn to operate wood-cutting machines.

_____

_____

_____

Unit 5 Jobs

3 Read these job advertisements and answer the questions below.

> **A** **Grape harvest**
> Our grapes are ready to harvest.
> We need additional pickers to help on the farm for the month of February.

> **B** **Machine operator – knitting factory**
> Knitting machine operator needed for new knitting factory.
> At least five years' experience.
> Must be prepared to work shifts.
> Excellent wages.

a) Which job is secondary work?

_____

b) How can technology be used to help with each type of work?

_____

_____

_____

_____

c) Which activity do you think will pay a higher wage? Why?

_____

_____

4 What jobs do people do at your school? Make a list.

_____

_____

_____

_____

_____

_____

Unit 6 Pollution

Lesson 1: Damaging the environment

1 Look at this picture carefully and answer the questions.

a) Make a list of all the things you can see in the picture that are polluting the street.

_____

_____

b) Where does this pollution come from?

_____

c) How does this type of pollution affect people and animals?

_____

_____

d) Which of the effects from question c) do you think is the most serious? Why?

_____

_____

Unit 6 **Pollution**

❷ Make a list of four other things that cause pollution on water, in the air or on land.

_____

_____

_____

_____

❸ Use this chart to record objects found in your home or at school. Find out the length of time they take to decay.

Give your chart a title which says where the objects were found.

_____

Name of object	What it is made of	Estimated time to decay
1.		
2.		
3.		
4.		
5.		
6.		

→ Supports Pupil Book Investigation, page 33

Unit 6 Pollution

Lesson 2: 'Green living'

1 Draw a diagram with pictures and labels to show ways in which people can help to reduce pollution. Use one of the diagram structures shown here.

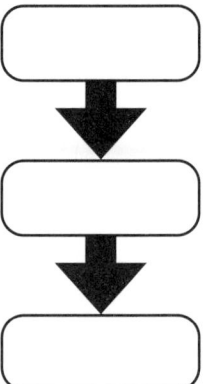

2 <u>Underline</u> three types of renewable energy.

energy from the sun

wind energy

hydropower (from water)

energy from burning oil and coal

Unit 6   Pollution

3 The three 'r's below are important for green living. Give an example of an action to go with each 'r' word. Draw a picture and write a sentence to explain it.

→ Supports Pupil Book Climate change, page 35

Reduce	
Reuse	
Recycle	

4 Write four ideas for your school's 'Waste and Pollution' policy that you can share with your class.

_____

_____

_____

_____

→ Supports Pupil Book Investigation, page 35

35

Unit 6 Pollution

Lesson 3: Exploring clean energy

1 Check your vocabulary knowledge by completing this quiz.

a) When this erupts, it sends lots of dust and poisonous gas into the air.

_____

b) This type of waste can take up to a million years to decay.

_____

c) Carbon _____ come from vehicles and factories that burn fossil fuels.

e) What do we call resources (such as wind energy) that will not run out?

_____

f) These flat things are often placed on the roofs of buildings to catch the energy of the sun and turn it into electricity.

_____

g) These machines change energy from water and the wind into electrical power.

_____

h) What can weed killer and washing powder contain that may be harmful to the environment?

_____

2 Add three more questions about pollution of your own. Ask a friend to answer them. (Make sure you know the answers.)

Question: _____

Answer: _____

Question: _____

Answer: _____

Question: _____

Answer: _____

Unit 6 Pollution

3 Think about your investigation into pollution in your local area. Use the information you gathered to answer the questions. Write in full sentences.

   a) What are the main types of pollution in your local area?

   _____

   _____

   b) What is the worst type of pollution in your local area?

   _____

   c) Is noise pollution a problem in your local area? Explain why you think it is or is not a problem.

   _____

   _____

   _____

4 Choose one other different type of pollution you found in your investigation.

   Type of pollution: _____ Survey score: ☐

   a) What causes this pollution?

   _____

   _____

   b) Why do you think this type of pollution is a problem for the local area?

   _____

   _____

   c) Suggest one way in which you can help to solve this problem.

   _____

   _____

→ Supports Pupil Book Investigation, page 37

Unit 7 Wales

Lesson 1: Mountains and valleys

1 a) Colour the word boxes to show:

    i) cities in pink   **ii)** mountains in yellow

    iii) rivers and channels in blue   **iv)** islands in green.

b) Write the words in the correct places on the map of Wales.

| Swansea | Bangor | Cambrian Mountains |

| River Wye | River Severn | Cardiff | Anglesey |

| Bristol Channel | Holyhead | Yr Wyddfa (Snowdon) |

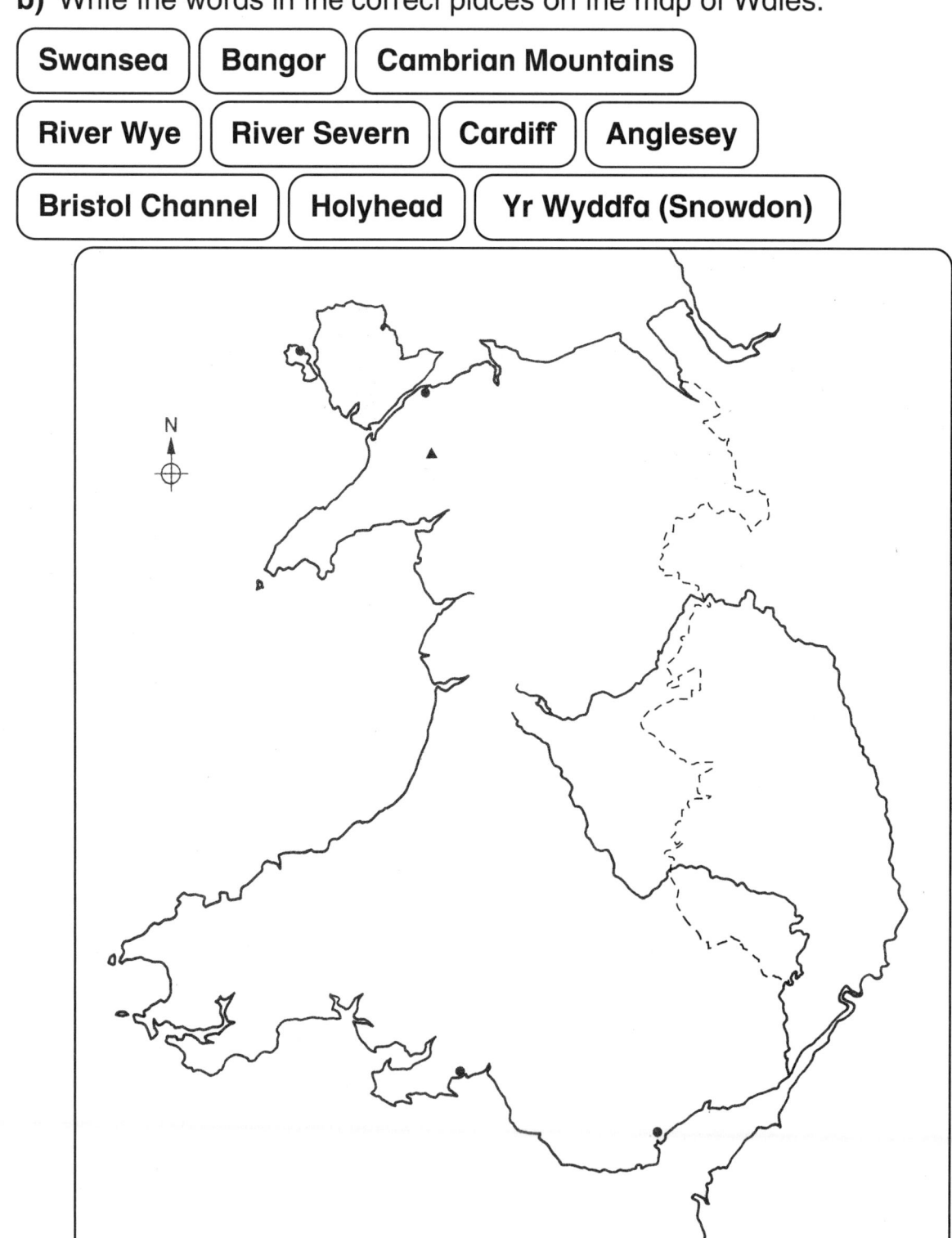

Unit 7 Wales

2 Compile a fact file about North Wales. Use the headings to fill in the information.

Fact file: North Wales

Weather	
Landscape	
Settlements	
Work	
Transport	

→ Supports Pupil Book Investigation, page 39

3 Find out two interesting facts about Cardiff, the capital of Wales.

_____

_____

4 Answer these questions about transport in Wales.

a) If you visited Holyhead and wanted to go to Ireland afterwards, which type of transport could you use?

_____

b) Which bridge would you cross if you travelled on the motorway between Wales and England?

_____

Unit 7 Wales

Lesson 2: The story of Blaenavon

1 Answer these questions about Blaenavon.

a) What does the name 'Blaenavon' mean in Welsh?

_____

b) Where is the town?

_____

c) What was the coal from the mine used for?

_____

d) What happened when ships and railways stopped using coal?

_____

e) How do people earn a living in Blaenavon today?

_____

2 Why is it not a good idea to burn coal as a source of energy? Write a paragraph, giving two reasons.

_____

_____

_____

_____

_____

_____

3 What was the Industrial Revolution? Colour in the best answer.

> A time when machines and factories were built to make goods more cheaply and more quickly.

> A time when people protested against the wealth and the power of factory owners.

Unit 7 Wales

4 Look at the information on pages 40 and 41 of your Pupil Book. Complete the timeline showing the history of Blaenavon.

  a) Look for the first date below in your Pupil Book. Write what happened on this date.

  b) Find five other dates and events to complete the timeline.

> **Hint:** Write the years in order on the timeline, from longest ago at the top to most recent at the bottom.

- 1789 • _____
- 1800 • Ironworks operating
- _____ • _____
- _____ • Very high demand for coal
- _____ • _____
- _____ • _____
- _____ • _____

→ Supports Pupil Book Investigation, page 41

Unit 7 Wales

Lesson 3: A visit to Big Pit

❶ Look at the diagram of a coal mine below. Label the diagram using these words:

| Pithead | Fan house | Down shaft | Ventilation doors | Coal face |

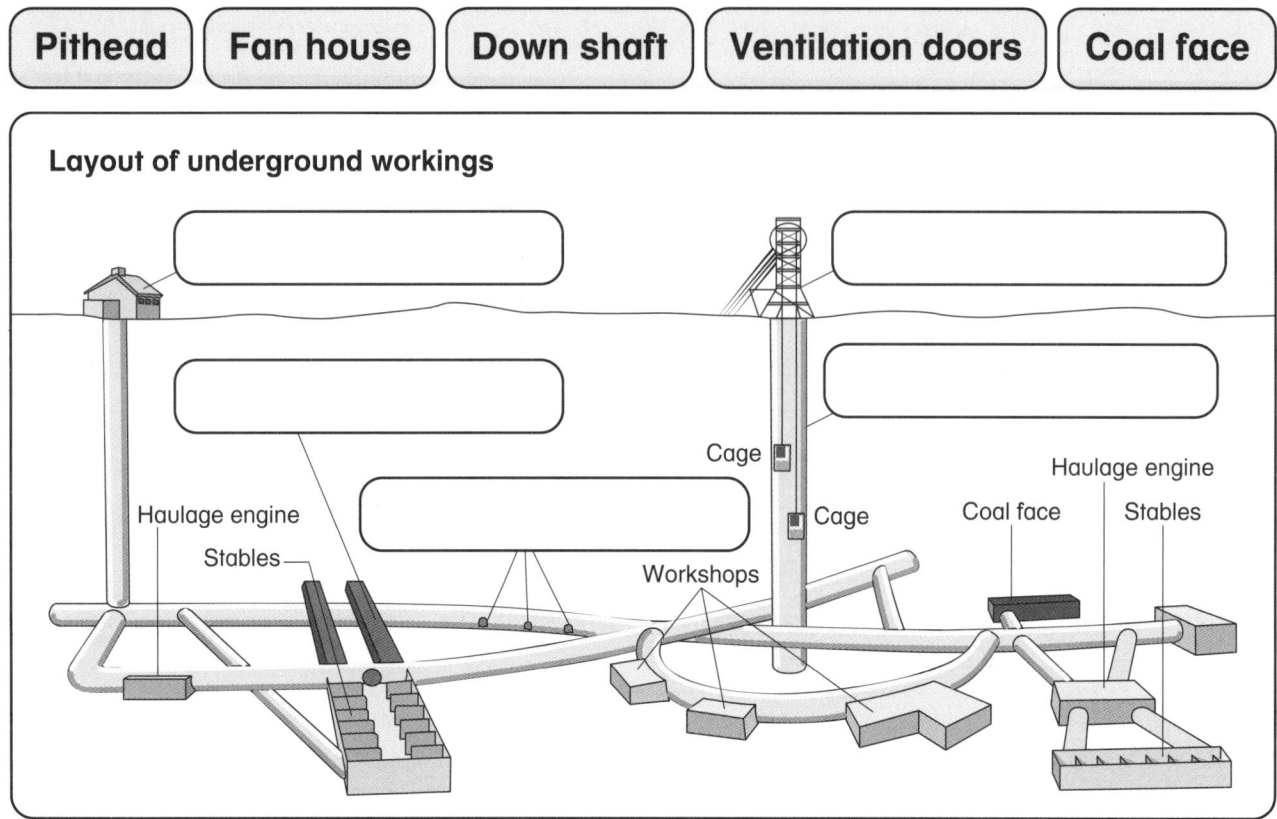

❷ What was it like to be a coal miner? Draw a picture or write a few sentences to show what coal miners wore and the work they did.

Unit 7 Wales

❸ Imagine that you are a tour guide. You need to tell a group of tourists three interesting facts about Big Pit that they will remember. What would you tell them?

_____

_____

_____

❹ Find or draw a picture of another World Heritage Site in your country or a country that you know. Write a sentence about why the site is important.

_____

_____

→ Supports Pupil Book Investigation, page 43

Unit 8   Greece

Lesson 1: Introducing Greece

1 Complete the map.

a) Colour in Greece.

b) Label the neighbouring countries.

c) Label these places:

Athens   Thessaloniki   Corinth Canal

Aegean Sea   Ionian Sea   Crete

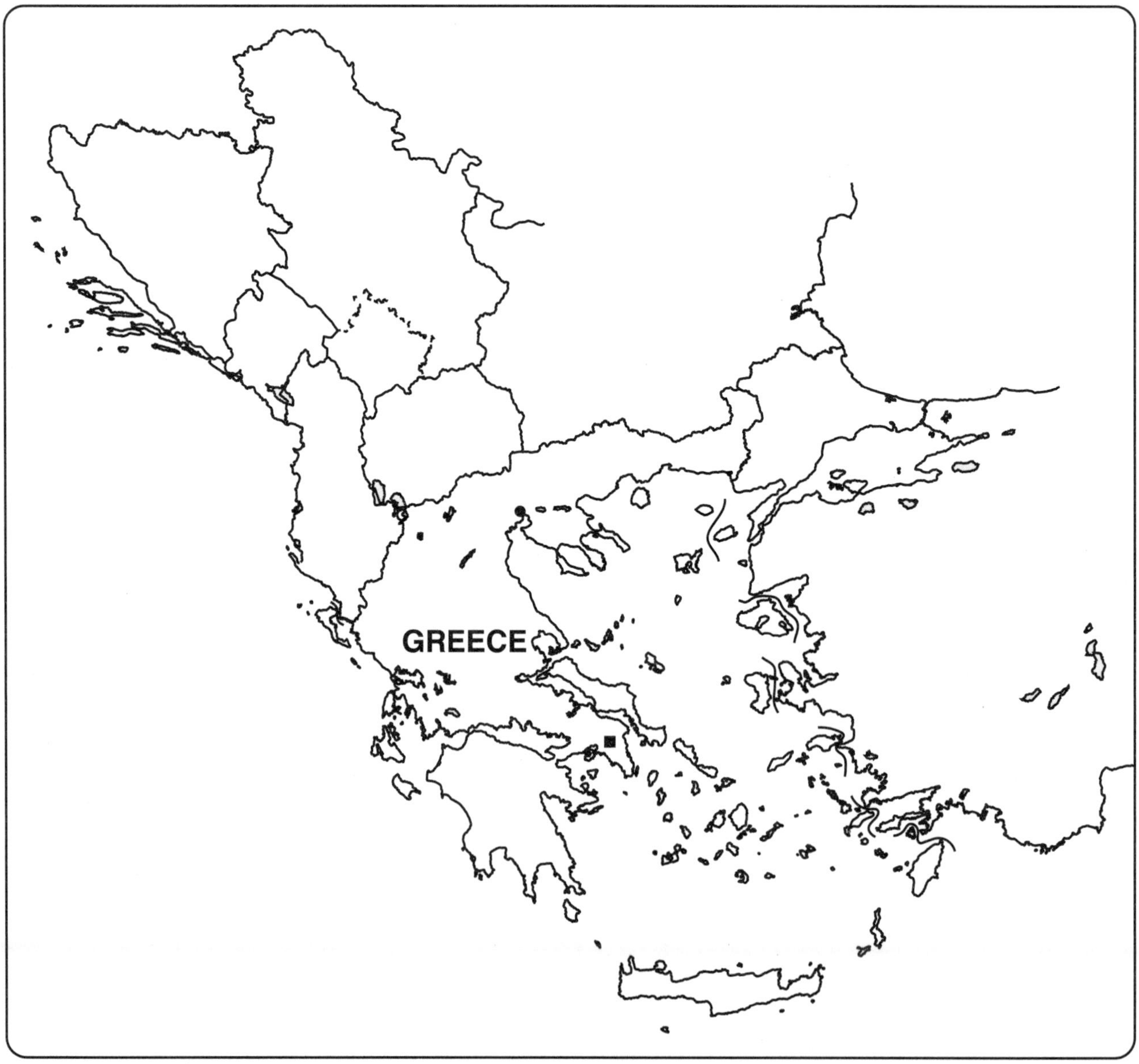

Unit 8 **Greece**

2 Make a fact file about Greece. Use the headings in the table to fill in the information.

Fact file: Greece

Climate	
Landscape	
Settlements	
Work	
Transport	

→ Supports Pupil Book Investigation, page 45

3 Look at your fact file about Greece and answer these questions.

a) Why do you think most people like to visit Greece from May to September?

_____

_____

b) How do people travel around the islands in Greece?

_____

c) How would you like to travel if you visited Greece? Why?

_____

_____

Unit 8 Greece

Lesson 2: Summer in Athens

1 Make a timeline of your own day, like Dimitra's timeline on page 46 of your Pupil Book.

Dimitra's day

Sleep	School	Lunch and sleep	Extra lessons	Play or watch TV	Sleep

Midnight　　　　　　　　8:00 a.m.　　　　　1:00 p.m.　　4:00 p.m. 6:00 p.m.　　　10:00 p.m. Midnight

My day

Midnight　　　　　　　　　　　　　　　　　　　　　　　　　　　　　　　　　Midnight

→ Supports Pupil Book Investigation, page 47

2 Look at this photograph of Athens and answer the questions.

a) Why do you think Athens needs 'pocket parks'?

_____

_____

b) How will pocket parks help the people who live in Athens?

_____

_____

Unit 8 Greece

❸ Reread page 47 of your Pupil Book, about the journey that Dimitra makes with her family to get the ferry at Piraeus.

a) Dimitra lives next to the museum and a park. Draw a circle on the map below to show where Dimitra's house might be.

b) Trace a possible route that Dimitra and her family could take from their house to Piraeus. Pass as many landmarks as possible.

c) Make a list of the landmarks they would pass if they followed your route.

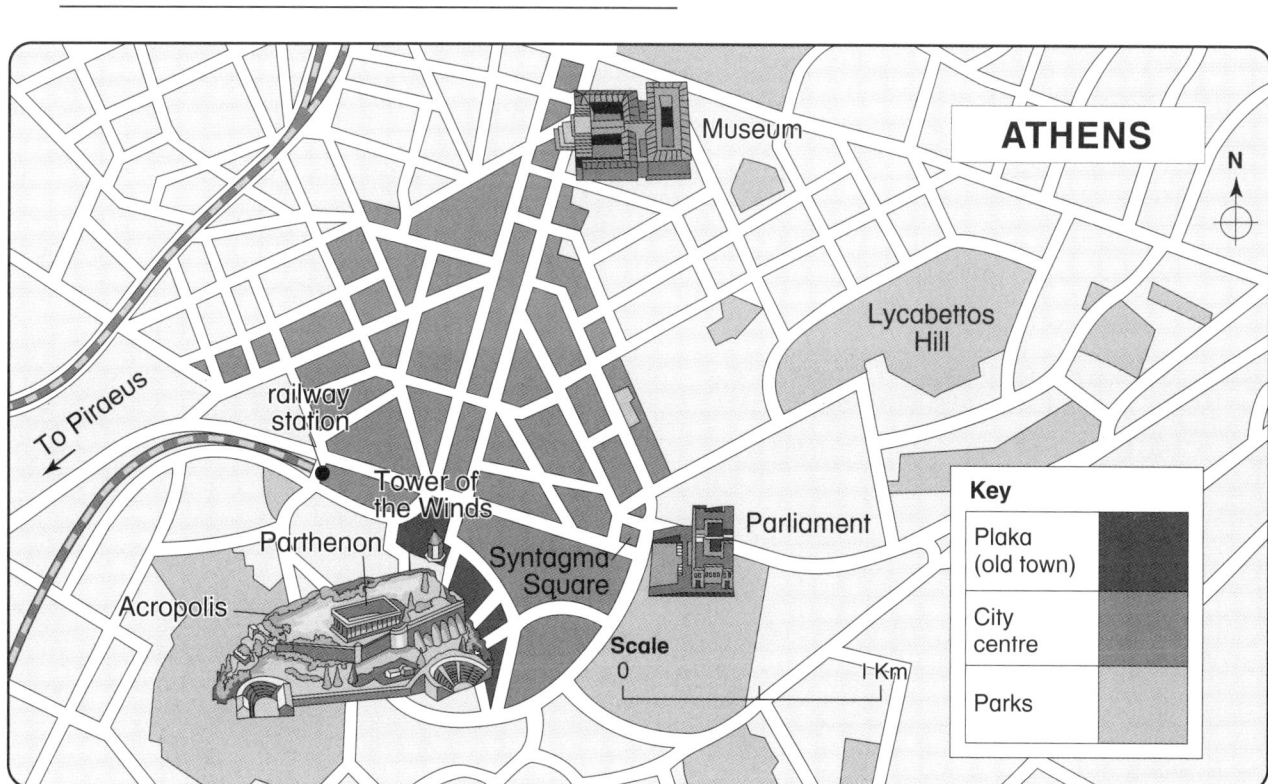

Unit 8 Greece

Lesson 3: A Greek island

1 Draw lines to match the words to their definitions.

beach	painted with white paint
ferry	a small restaurant
whitewashed	a town or city on the coast with a harbour
port	a small green or black fruit, used to make cooking oil
taverna	a piece of land covered with sand or pebbles next to the sea
olives	a boat or a ship that carries passengers and goods across short distances

2 a) Use an atlas to find the names of more islands in Greece. Write the names of six islands you would like to visit.

_____   _____

_____   _____

_____   _____

b) Plan a trip to the Greek islands using the table below. How will you get from one place to another? Start in Athens, at the port or airport.

Hint: Think about ...
- how long the ferry or plane takes
- which way of travel is cheaper
- which way of travel is best for the environment.

From	To	Transport
Athens		

Unit 8   Greece

❸ This is an outline of the island of Amorgos.

   a) Draw a route map for tourists who want to travel from Tholaria to Katapola by bus.

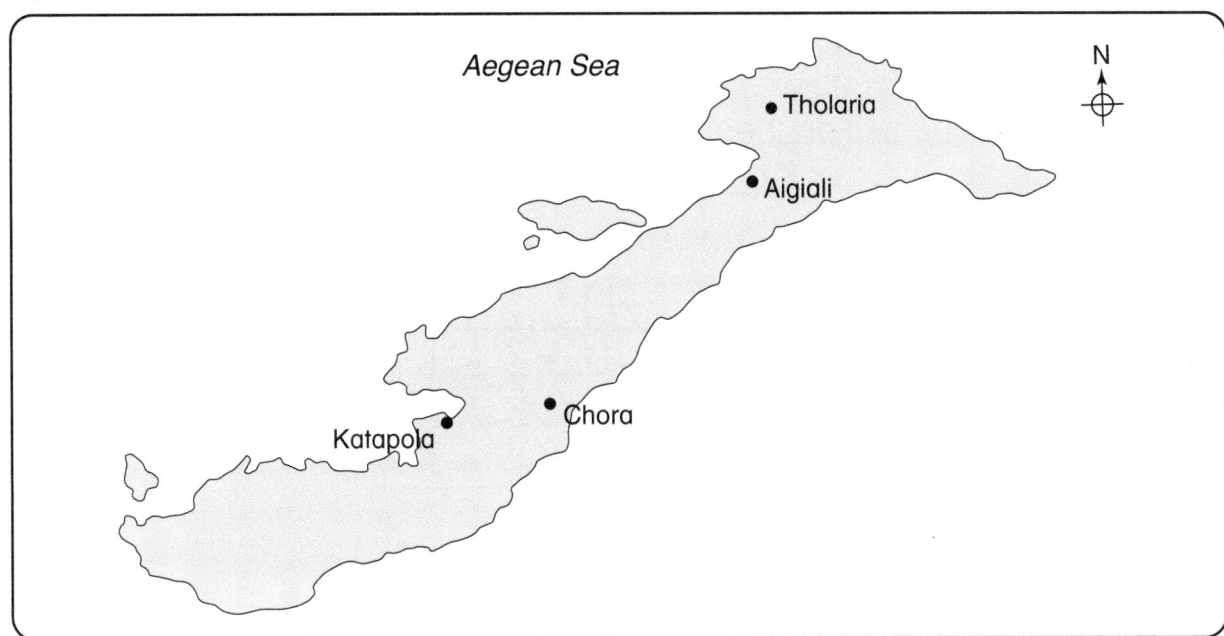

→ Supports Pupil Book Mapwork, page 49

   b) Write two or three sentences for the tourists to describe what they might see on the way.

   _____
   _____
   _____
   _____
   _____

❹ What would you like to do and see if you visited Amorgos?

   _____
   _____
   _____
   _____
   _____
   _____

Unit 9 North America

Lesson 1: Introducing the Caribbean

❶ Find a map of the Caribbean which shows the names of many of the islands.

a) Find nine Caribbean islands in the wordsearch puzzle.

b) Check the names on the map or in an atlas.

q	A	p	f	J	T	C	u	b	a
B	n	t	w	a	r	g	m	y	z
a	t	c	x	m	i	s	T	h	k
H	i	s	p	a	n	i	o	l	a
a	g	u	j	i	i	j	b	k	x
m	u	z	f	c	d	b	a	n	j
a	a	o	y	a	a	d	g	p	q
s	x	h	w	n	d	b	o	i	k
g	S	t	L	u	c	i	a	z	z
M	a	r	t	i	n	i	q	u	e

❷ Look at this photograph of St Vincent and the Grenadines in the Caribbean.
Why do you think tourists like to visit this place? Write a list.

Unit 9 North America

3 Complete these sentences. Use the words from the boxes.

| Cancer | reggae | Antilles | French | tropical |

a) Cuba is near the Tropic of _____.

b) Jamaica is part of an island chain called the Greater _____.

c) The Caribbean has a _____ climate.

d) English, Spanish and _____ are some of the languages spoken in the Caribbean.

e) The Caribbean is famous for rap and _____ music.

4 What do you know about hurricanes?

a) Find the answers to these questions and make notes in the table.

b) Use the last two rows to write any additional information that you find.

Hurricanes

What is a hurricane?	
What causes a hurricane?	
At what speed does the wind blow during a hurricane?	
Where do hurricanes occur?	
What routes do hurricanes take in the Caribbean?	
What damage do hurricanes do?	

→ Supports Pupil Book Investigation, page 51

Unit 9 North America

Lesson 2: Finding out about Jamaica

1 a) Fill in as much information as you can on this map of Jamaica.

For example, you can include place names, mountains and rivers.

b) Write words in the space around the map that describe Jamaica's landscape, culture, environment and climate. Use different colours to write words for each of these four categories.

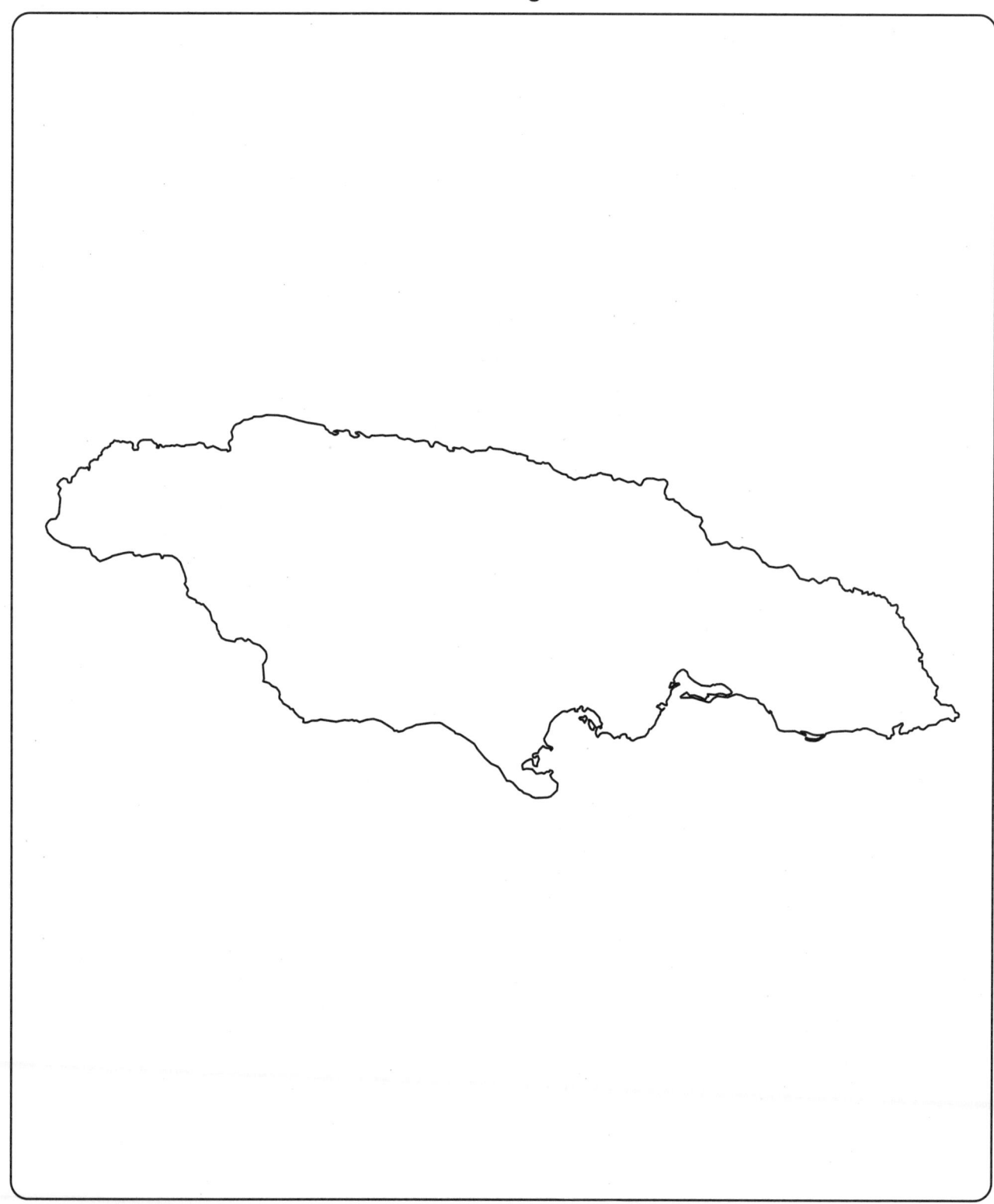

Unit 9 **North America**

2 Find or draw a landscape in Jamaica that interests you.

3 Write three short paragraphs with facts and information about Jamaica. Include information about the:
- landscape
- climate
- economy (crops, mining and manufacturing).

_____

_____

_____

_____

_____

_____

_____

_____

_____

_____

_____

_____

Unit 9 — North America

Lesson 3: Living in Jamaica

1 a) Reread pages 53 to 55 of your Pupil Book. Draw a picture of the house and surrounding area in Jamaica where Ingrid Morrison grew up.

Here are some things you could include:

- bungalow
- verandah
- sugar cane
- sweet potatoes
- palm trees
- orchard

b) Write two or three sentences about what Ingrid Morrison's life in Jamaica was like as a child.

_____

_____

_____

_____

c) How has Claremont changed since Ingrid was a child?

_____

_____

Unit 9 North America

❷ Make a fact file about Jamaica. Think about which headings to include. Use this chart: add your headings and ideas.

➜ Supports Pupil Book Investigation, page 55

Unit 10 Africa

Lesson 1: Introducing Africa

1 a) Colour the key.

Key			
mountain ☐	desert ☐	grassland ☐	forest ☐

b) Now use your key and colour the map to show the mountain, desert, grassland and forest areas in Africa.

Unit 10 Africa

Quiz time! How much do you know about Africa?

❷ First answer these questions.

a) Which desert covers a large part of Africa?
_____

b) What happened to African lands in the 19th century?
_____

c) True or false? Coffee and cobalt are exported from Africa.
_____

d) Is the Nile the largest lake in Africa?
_____

e) Is the area around the equator forest or grassland?
_____

f) Name one city in Africa that is on the coast.
_____

❸ Now write 10 questions of your own about Africa to ask others in your class.

1. _____
2. _____
3. _____
4. _____
5. _____
6. _____
7. _____
8. _____
9. _____
10. _____

→ Supports Pupil Book Investigation, page 57

Unit 10 Africa

Lesson 2: Learning about Kenya

1 Complete the map of Kenya below by adding this information.

a) The name of the capital city.

b) The name of a big lake in the north.

c) The name of the ocean on the east coast.

d) The name of the river that runs into the ocean on the east coast.

e) The name of a desert in the north of Kenya.

2 Colour in the key with the colours specified. Then colour in the map to show the areas given in the key.

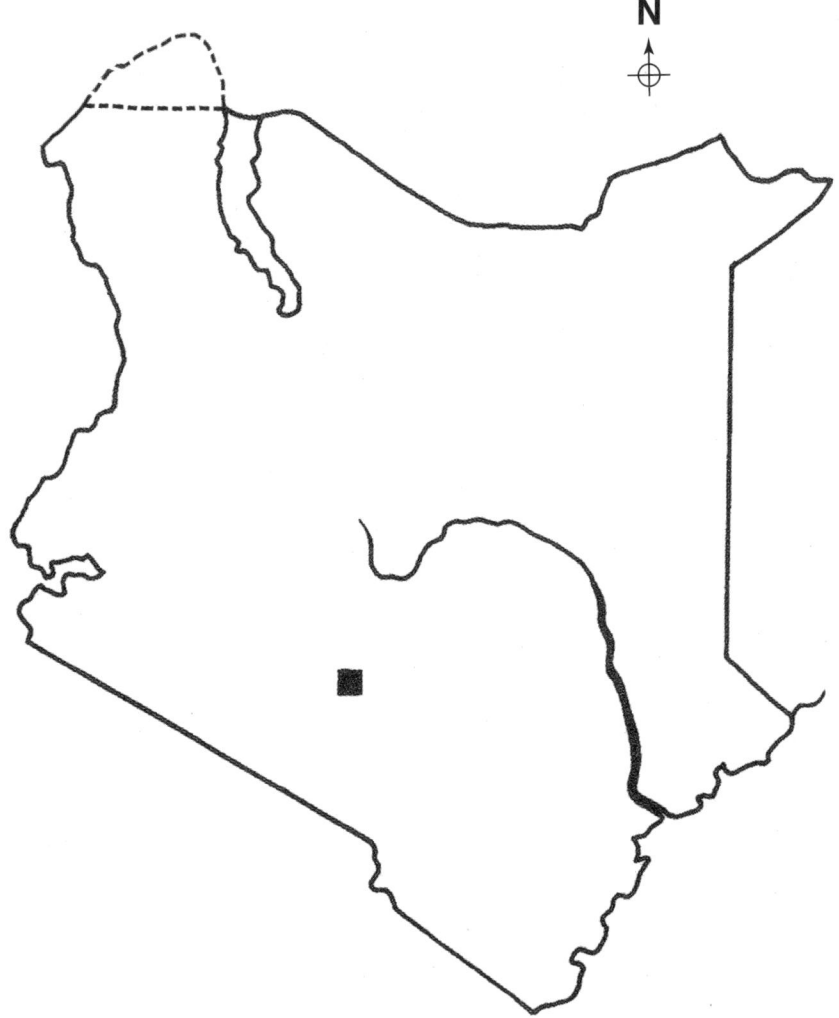

Key

Over 1000 metres		orange
200–1000 metres		yellow
0–200 metres		green

Unit 10 Africa

3 a) Reread page 59 of your Pupil Book. Write a short description of Miriam's life in your own words. Use these headings.

Home and family

_____

_____

_____

Hobbies

_____

_____

_____

School day

_____

_____

_____

→ Supports Pupil Book Investigation, page 59

b) How is your life different from Miriam's life?

_____

_____

4 What objects would you put in a box to describe your life? Draw six things.

Unit 10 Africa

Lesson 3: Living in Kenya

❶ Complete the paragraphs about how Kenya is changing. Use the words from the boxes.

| floods | homes | desert | climate |

| droughts | Mombasa | game | roses |

Recently, the rainfall patterns in Kenya have been different as a result of _____ change. Some areas have had _____ while other areas have had _____ because of very heavy rainfall. There are more _____ areas due to droughts.

Cities such as Nairobi and _____ have grown as people move to cities to look for work. The tourists who visit Kenya enjoy visiting _____ parks. But animals take up a lot of space which is also needed for _____ and growing crops. Crops such as beans and _____, which are exported, use a lot of water.

❷ Many farmers in Kenya keep cattle. Some farmers are **nomadic**, which means they move around with their cattle looking for food for the cattle to eat. How do you think tourism and climate change can affect their way of life?

_____

_____

_____

Unit 10 Africa

❸ Design an advertisement to attract tourists to Kenya.
Plan the information you will include. Make notes.

a) Where is Kenya?
_____
_____

b) What is the weather like?
_____
_____

c) How can tourists get there?
_____
_____

d) What would the tourists want to see?
_____
_____

e) What picture(s) would you put on the advertisement?
_____
_____

f) What sentence would you write at the top to attract the tourists?
_____
_____

→ Supports Pupil Book Investigation, page 61

Notes

William Collins' dream of knowledge for all began with the publication of his first book in 1819.

A self-educated mill worker, he not only enriched millions of lives, but also founded a flourishing publishing house. Today, staying true to this spirit, Collins books are packed with inspiration, innovation and practical expertise.
They place you at the centre of a world of possibility and give you exactly what you need to explore it.

Published by Collins
An imprint of HarperCollins*Publishers*
The News Building, 1 London Bridge Street, London, SE1 9GF, UK

HarperCollins*Publishers*
Macken House, 39/40 Mayor Street Upper, Dublin 1, D01 C9W8, Ireland

Browse the complete Collins catalogue at
collins.co.uk

© HarperCollins*Publishers* Limited 2025
Maps © Collins Bartholomew 2025
New York map on p23 created by Jouve

10 9 8 7 6 5 4 3 2 1

ISBN 978-0-00-872838-0

All rights reserved. No part of this publication may be reproduced, stored in a retrieval system, or transmitted in any form by any means, electronic, mechanical, photocopying, recording or otherwise, without the prior written permission of the Publisher or a licence permitting restricted copying in the United Kingdom issued by the Copyright Licensing Agency Ltd, 5th Floor, Shackleton House, 4 Battle Bridge Lane, London SE1 2HX.

Without limiting the author's and publisher's exclusive rights, any unauthorised use of this publication to train generative artificial intelligence (AI) technologies is expressly prohibited. HarperCollins also exercise their rights under Article 4(3) of the Digital Single Market Directive 2019/790 and expressly reserve this publication from the text and data mining exception.

British Library Cataloguing-in-Publication Data

A catalogue record for this publication is available from the British Library.

Author: Daphne Paizee
Publisher: Laura White
Product managers: Natasha Paul and Shelley Teasdale
Development editor: Judith Walters
Copyeditor: Catherine Dakin
Proofreader: Charlotte Christensen
Cover designer and illustrator: Steve Evans
Internal illustrator: Jouve India Private Ltd
Typesetter: David Jimenez
Production controller: Katie Jean-Baptiste
Printed and bound in the UK by Martins the Printers

This book is produced from independently certified FSC™ paper to ensure responsible forest management.

For more information visit: www.harpercollins.co.uk/green
collins.co.uk/sustainability

Acknowledgements

The publishers gratefully acknowledge the permission granted to reproduce the copyright material in this book. Every effort has been made to trace copyright holders and to obtain their permission for the use of copyright material. The publishers will gladly receive any information enabling them to rectify any error or omission at the first opportunity.

All photos: Shutterstock.